BLIND HORSE

POEMS

JEANNE BRYNER

Working Lives Series
Bottom Dog Press
Huron, Ohio

Cover Art: "Settlement" by Wanda Kover

ACKNOWLEDGMENTS

Grateful acknowledgment is made to the following publications in which these poems first appeared sometimes in slightly different form: "Apple Chunks," *Best of 1991* Ohio Poetry Day; "Coons," "Paper Dolls," and "The End of It," *The Wittenberg Review*; "Delivery Men," *Plainsongs*; "Gray Fox" and "Ice Cream," *5 AM*; "Homesick," *Lullwater Review*; "How to Say It" and "Snow Horses," *Ohio Poetry Review*; "The Story of My Village," *Tantra Press*; "Number One" and "Madera Canyon, Walking With My Sister," *Texas Journal of Women and the Law*; "Thunder," *Earth's Daughters*; "Road From West Virginia," *Sou'wester*; "Kick the Can," *Poem*; "Steel Blues," *New Kent Quarterly*; "Sunday Morning," **Hiram Poetry Review**; "The 400 Block, 1954," *Manna*; "The Mill's Annual Picnic, 1960: Conneaut Lake Park, PA," *Cream City Review*; "Trains," *The Sun*; "Why It Happens," *Poetry East*; "Under A Funeral Canopy in Rockingham, NC," *Black Warrior Review*; "Blood Sisters," *Midland Review*; "Pizza," *Canto*; "My Grandmother's Engagement," *Kent State University Wick Poetry*; "Breeding," "Coal Miner, Caples, WV, 1938," and "Our Fathers," *Getting By: Stories of Working Lives*(Bottom Dog Press, 1996); "Desert Flowers," *Down the River: An Anthology of Ohio Valley Fiction and Poetry* (Cincinnati: Cincinnati Landing of Always a River, 1991); "On the Rocks," *Mahoning Valley Poetry* (Cleveland: Bacchae Press, 1993); "Where God Lives," *What's Become of Eden: Poems of Family at Century's End* (New York: Slapering Hol Press, 1994); "Lourdes," *West Branch*; "How Steel Shapes Our Lives: Grade Two, Arlington Elementary," *Learning by Heart* (Iowa City: Iowa UP, 1999); "Sunday Morning" and "Our Fathers," *Boomer Girls: American Women Poets Come of Age* (Iowa City: Iowa UP, 1999); "Where Animals Gather," *Dickinson Review*; "Art in the Mill" and "The Devotion of Brown Lives" *Calliope*; "Coal Miner's Daughter, 1933" and "Letter to West Virginia," *Journal of Kentucky Studies*; and "What Happened in the Fire Drill," *Nebo*.

I would like to express my appreciation to Robert Wick and Walter Wick for providing Kent State University with the Stan and Tom Wick Poetry Scholarship program. The heart of this manuscript was written after my trip to Bisbee, Arizona, in 1990. More poems were written in 1992 while I was at Bucknell University, Lewisburg, Pennsylvania, with the Seminar for Younger Poets Fellowship program. I thank Mr. Jack Stadler for providing this opportunity. After receiving a 1997 Individual Artist Fellowship from the Ohio Arts Council, more than a dozen new poems were written for this manuscript. I thank the Ohio Arts Council for the vote of confidence and the fellowship.

For typing this manuscript several times during its long evolution I thank my neighbor, Sally Macklin. For supporting early writing endeavors and commenting on this manuscript, I would like to thank the following people: Elizabeth Hoobler, Gloria Young, Vivian Pemberton, Gary Ciuba, Mary Ann Lowry, Mary Turzillo, Sanford Marovitz, Susanna Fein, Robin Becker, Brigit Kelly, and Colette Inez. And special thanks to Maggie Anderson for her friendship, scholarship, and common sense.

I thank David, Gary, Lisa, Summar, Tony, Ashley, and Joe for their circle of love and the space to create. Special thanks to Summar for teaching me some basic computer skills for this book and other manuscripts.

Bottom Dog Press
c/o Firelands College
Huron, Ohio 44839
419-433-5560 Lsmithdog@aol.com

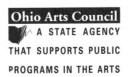

Ohio Arts Council
A STATE AGENCY
THAT SUPPORTS PUBLIC
PROGRAMS IN THE ARTS

For my family and all families who have thrown
trunks and dishes from wagons
so the horses could make it to the river.

They went in their simplicity, and they knew not anything.
II Samuel, 15:11

TABLE OF CONTENTS

The blind horse is fittest for the mill.

— Maid's Last Prayer.
Act iii, sc1.
Thomas Southerne

Stonehenge

Our mill stands by the river
where all the men have disappeared.
In July sunlight, air hangs like a shroud.
Everything inside and outside
has come to a stop: furnace, pulleys, rails.

In the grass at my feet
gray rocks in a near circle
their roundness smooth as skulls
arranging themselves
bringing their hands up
to shield their sockets.

Road From West Virginia

I.
A cock crows, and it's Wednesday morning.
Father wakes, face peppered, stiff with stubble.
His breath's a honky-tonk armpit.
He tells mama to pack her babies.
A lotus in a calico duster, snaps undone, she sits
and brushes the sun's silky space through
hollows of her honey brown hair.
Behind her, he ticks in the oval mirror.
Gray smoke rises from his cigarette
like a snake's ghost, and he's Houdini
with black curls, explaining their escape.

What he says: *Fast money, big money.*
Honey, farm boys are dinosaurs, coal mines
are tar pits. Ohio, and the steel mills
that's where we're going.

II.
Friday night, cicadas sing, and mama sleeps
in her great-grandmother's ivory poster bed.
She dreams her hair is a horse,
a mare running from a burning barn,
she chases the flaming mane
clear to the dogwoods of White Creek.
Water breaks, her face, swollen and azure,
swirls up, eyes blank under thick ice.

What she hears: *The Union. My brother,*
Virgil, works graveyard. Ohio, the red mills
that's where we're going to.

III.
Sunday. Father pulls grandmother from her cornfield
and says, *I'm taking Mary and them babies,*
they'll travel with me, tonic bottles for my wagon,
promise blankets for my bed. Grandmother leans
her crepe neck on the hoe, studies signs in tendrils
of wandering pumpkin vines, reads winter's harness
in his charcoal eyes.

What she sees: *Thunder comes, rides a narrow saddle.*
His ring's her rein. Ohio, the bloody mills,
that's where they're going to die.

Moving Horses

found poem by J. F. Kelly
horse dealer

The working of a horse's mind
is not easy to understand
but, in my opinion, fear

rather than stubbornness
is at the root of the trouble.
It may not be generally realized

how many horses suffer
from claustrophobia and are terrified
when forced to enter a confined space.

The hollow and unfamiliar sound
of his feet on the ramp and floor
of the box upsets some horses.

To him it is probably a warning
that the surface
will not bear his weight.

On the Rocks

You'd see them on ritual rocks
by the rust-rimmed river at breaktime.
Blue cotton sleeves, steaming red thermos,
white bread sandwiches, and black mayonnaise cake

sliced thick, like their women.
Their silver buckets opened in a yawn.
They hound-dog stretched and chewed
on grass blades after they ate

and watched the gypsy river lull and loaf.
Their backs to the mill, they spoke
their dreams in chants against the breast
of summer, they beat their wives in fits

against the crush of debt, and they doused
their springtime fire against the neck of whiskey.
You'd see them on altar rocks — melted men
of steel — their backs to the mill.

Steel Blues

The mill was Dachau
and our fathers
were the Jews
and the soap
was a paycheck
and their numbers
were herds
and their language
was silence
and red ovens
were bubbling
and the screams
were wives
and the days
were razors
and the children
were yokes
and their sweat
floated barges
and their ashes
are dust
on rich men's lapels
and their cough
is a gum wad
on gold high heels.
And the mill
has closed
and our fathers
are smoke
and we
let it breathe
for now
forever
we remember
the cost of blue steel.

The 400 Block, 1954

Five ponytails at a time
we'd squeeze inside musty, oil breath
coal bins — our summer playhouses.
Black smudge tea parties and milk white
grins and one-eyed baby dolls with no hair.
And us, hard as ebony coal, waiting in our den,
wanting to be diamonds.

Ice Cream

Summer steeped and pulled
the sky blue ice cream truck
to our side of town where kids
were sand and money was magic.

We'd hear its wind chime song
grow stronger as it kissed the curves
of every block. We could taste vanilla
buried under bitter chocolate,
sweet melting sugar cream frozen fast to a stick.

Summer steeped and pulled
our fathers to hell's oven
at the mill, and we all got angry
because that brazen ice cream truck
still came, still came day after day.

It still came knowing that sweet dream
stuff, that fine cool flavor
was out of reach
for our gingham mothers.

Summer steeped and pulled
its trigger with little bullets pressed
to little brains. It was the sky blue
ice cream truck, a wind chime song
growing weaker as it kissed the curves of every block.

Kick the Can

We played kick the can.
What was supposed to be our playground
was two scrub lots they forgot
to slap up houses on during the war.

Weeds were too high for the kids,
ticks from dogs, deep ruts from never
being tilled, and broken whiskey necks
crouched low like our folks' dreams.

When they mowed, we had two wooden swings
drooping like our mothers in nameless
red bandanas. Grimy, coal-dust brats,
we grabbed them, fought over them,
punched each other, trying to claim
their lap for our own.

There were three pipes soldered together
shaped like the tops of our iron fisted fathers,
both hands buried in sorry dirt,
fingers mashed in mud, arms of steel curving
at the shoulders, headless nobodies falling
back to the ground.

We swarmed those pipes that once held
mystic teeter totters, rotted so long ago
only Tommy Braden's brother, Jeff, remembered
they were painted orange, and we believed him.

Sun beat against our backs
like it does on little clouds, and our darkness,
our shadows grew bigger and badder every season.

How Steel Shapes Our Lives:
Grade Two, Arlington Elementary

Our teacher, Mrs. Dillon, raises
the square white screen.
It might be a sail wanting wind
or our mothers' pale sheets
trying to dry in January.

This is Ohio 1958.
This, our third year away from West Virginia
and the forsythia by the farmhouse.
This is assembly: gray chairs, a movie
about How Steel Shapes Our Lives.
We are small, our hands folded.

Mornings of walking to the barn
with my grandfather are far away.
Still, lambs crying for dead mothers
must be bottle fed. I know it
and know how, when they suck,
it feels good to pet their wet faces.

Mr. Jonah makes the room go dark,
then, he flips a switch: magic, magic.
A light warms the reel's black film,
upside-down numbers flash. We hear
a big voice without a face.

We have been taught to sit and listen.
The movie makes us feel like we're beside
the men in hard hats, where yellow dozers
gouge the earth, take what they want,
haul it to our mills for processing.

This is the inside of a steel mill, the voice says.
We watch the men move like shadows on the screen.
These are the stories given to children:

evil trolls beneath the bridge, to cross over
someone must pay a toll or be eaten.

This is a blast furnace, the big voice says.
We don't even know what that means,
but a pink glow settles on our faces
as the ladle vomits its river of red steel.
Sparks spray the men's coveralls, hands,
and hair — men who look like Tom's father,

Debbie's father, my father, so I whisper
Run, Run, Run, and rub my Bible-school
Jesus pin for luck. But, there's so much noise
in the mill, the men can't hear me.
They wear their iron shoes
and keep walking through the fire.

What Happened in the Fire Drill

for Mrs. Amy Davis

Gypsy Lane, snow past the bumper of father's Buick,
Mama, in her hospital gown, again, crying, depressed.
Doc Mason mumbles, *give her three shock treatments*
and *No, I don't think she's pregnant.* Inside mama
my baby brother's a tadpole, a secret floating in a pink ocean.
Then, the lightning zaps him, snaps him, slaps him. He tries
to swim away, the cord wraps his neck, one, two, three times.
He waits to be cut loose, grows heavy, Raggedy Andy hangs
himself on a bloody branch.

Blue baby, incubator, *we don't know if he'll live.*
My grandmother says name him from the Bible, call him
Benjamin. My folks, numb, press the nursery's window.
Mama cries; father holds her hand. Doctors say *cerebral palsy.*
Ben's cerebellum's a drunken cowboy in town for a Saturday
night that lasts forever. Pabulum chokes him, he can't sit alone.
Dish towels strap him in the maple high chair until he's four.
He bites his tongue, likes strawberry ice cream and bananas.
We all carry him; when he runs, his feet are broken paddle wheels.
Bobby Ford calls him *retard*, gets a willow limb across his backside
when we tell his mama.

First grade. Ben sits, patient at his varnished ink-well desk,
blonde hair shaved close, green pullover, wide eyes of a fawn.
He repeats numbers, colors, slobbers, wipes his chin.
Stars in the flag. He stands, covers his heart.
Outside the long windows, the football field's shoulders lie
pinned by heavy goal posts.

His teacher smiles, slim in her lavender suit and light pearls,
straight like Ben's teeth. Her chiffon blouse exhales *White Shoulders,*
White Shoulders. Ivory pumps and sable hair in a French twist,
she's Lady Bird Johnson with chalk dust
on her fingertips, apples on her desk.

Ben squints, no end to his papers' blue lines.
No letting up. No pause. The trick is to get letters to land
between these lines. He knows this. For years he's seen
his sisters dash from the yawning school bus waving
math exams, spelling tests, manila papers filled with gold stars,
big red A's. His pencil becomes a black frog licking
his squat fingers and spastic hands. He bites the left side
of his tongue, it's an anchor, something to make
his *B* stay put.

Fifth grade, row three, Mrs. Barrick reads us
the *Little House* books, raw blizzards, how families survive.
Her voice feels like the hearth in their sod house.
And I think orange flames dancing. I wonder
how Ben will ride out a fire drill with a drunk cowboy
in his brain. I imagine him tumbling down the stairs,
trampled by polished Buster Browns and dirty saddle shoes.
I'm way up here where Laura's sister's going blind.
I'm on the second floor, where I can't see Ben or carry him.

Fire drill. A wail like a man with a nailed hand.
I run from those prairie stories, fly down the hall,
remember smell of hair burning, I want to save
my baby brother who cannot run, who is not a retard.
I slip past the fourth grade teacher's clip board,
trip on a number two pencil, hit the gray steps
two at a time. When I round Ben's hallway, breathless,
I see his head bobbing like a sand balloon above
the lavender shoulder of Mrs. Davis
while she carries him
                    down
                        every
                            single
                                step
in those ivory pumps, his lead-smeared palms
rubbing her chiffon blouse, his saliva
glistening on her pearls.

Blood Sisters

Beth and Tammy Rae made it out
of the neighborhood before puberty.
And while we were learning how many
pennies it took to make a dime buy

a pack of Juicy Fruit and rolling Buglar
cigarettes for our folks, they were learning
how many beats to a measure. Their hands
grew soft and touched ivory keys.

Their bodies grew ruffly pink tutus.
And when they came to school, they forgot
our West Virginia names, how our butts blazed
diarrhea after six bowls of green cherries

from Purdy's tree, how we shared mud pies
and quilt tents, scratched our wrists with twigs,
lit a candle with stolen matches, and circle sat
under Taylor's porch, called ourselves, *Blood Sisters.*

We promised we'd always love each other —
dirty hugs, dirty lies. While we learned to inhale
our fathers' Camels and let the boys warm our lives
by holding our titties, they were voted *Prom Queen.*

And when they floated past us, prettier than Cinderella,
we waved our scarred wrists like windmills,
but their white gloves hid the beginning
and waltzed the other way.

Where God Lives

It is hard to believe in God, even now.
He was always somewhere else.
Maybe fishing. And sometimes I get mad.
Like when my sister was eight
and I was six. Daddy went drinking,
left us all alone with my baby brothers.
We were potty-training the chubby one, Ben.

I went to pull him off his potty seat
and his weenie got caught in a crack
of blue plastic. Blood spurted as if I'd
chopped a hen's neck. My sister ran.
All four of us crying now, and me holding
Ben's poor wiener
like a bloody worm in a washcloth.

I begged God to stop warm ooze soaking
through to my palm, and held Ben,
who yelped louder that Sam the day
we shut his tail in a closet. *I'm sorry,*
please God, help us. I chanted my prayer,
the way you do when you see the train's face
frothing in the tracks, yellow eyes and teeth
hissing the dark, and your car's stalled,
all the doors locked tight.

Our screen door whined, slammed,
when my sister brought the women
in their gingham blouses. They found Vaseline
in our cupboards, rocked Ben until he slept,
gave us orange popsicles, threw
the potty seat in the trash.

It is difficult to believe in God, even now,
but I want to say that day, when I was six
and holding what was left of my brother's dick

in my right hand, God's hair was in pin curls
under a red bandana. He had two names:
Elsie and Janet May. He lived on our street:
the four hundred block in the projects.
He was home; it was August and too hot for trout.

She had some horses she loved.
She had some horses she hated.

These were the same horses.

— *"She Had Some Horses"*
Joy Harjo

Fields and Clearings

To fill the empty space
there's a story you tell,
how your mama was a doe,
her eyes large and brown and sad.

In one photo, her shoulders draped
in velvet. People wonder why you travel
backwards, you explain *adaptive value,*
a new term to describe survival.

Deer do not have language,
but just the same they communicate
by signs and gestures. Wandering,
they cross highways and get hit.

Now, summer is nearly gone,
you remember her pacing the small house,
saying, *please take us for a drive,*
your father starts the blue Nash.

All the car windows remain down,
and your brothers' and sisters' voices sound
like water rising in a stream. At the edge
of town, he'll shut the engine off, tell us

hush, hush, so mama can watch
the deer eating grass behind the fence.
Winter's yard lies ahead,
and any clover that tastes like home

might just keep her from starving.

Letter to West Virginia
January 20, 1954

Dear Mom, My belly's big as a wash tub. This one's a boy for sure —
kicks me night and day. I'll call him same as his Daddy. Only thing more
tired than me is my elastic. For three weeks my underpants have been
acting just like Aunt Clara's parlor blinds. I pull them up and two min-
utes later they curl down tighter than a new perm under the south end of
this baby. The burn is healing on little Katie's arm, just pink now, the
scab fell off Friday. All morning Sam whimpered at the door. His water
froze solid as a kiss on a frosty window, and he could barely wag his tail.
We let him into the kitchen until Melvin gets home from the mill. There's
nothing here to hitch this blue wind to but skinny brown telephone poles.
The mill spits black specks on the snow, like too much pepper on mashed
potatoes. I never saw the like of flat stuff, squeezed-in families, hardly
any trees, and winter's hanging on stronger than a dead pole cat. Karen
Sue and Lee Ann both have colds, coughed until two this morning. I
rubbed them down with *Vicks* salve. I hope to ride to the A&P tomorrow
with Martha. I'm almost out of bleach and cornmeal. Tell Lucy and George
we ate the last of the blackberry jam. Sure miss picking with Lucy on
Pumpkin Run. Kiss Dad for me and keep your feet up. I know your legs
have been swelling. Thelma wrote and told me.
Love, Mary Elizabeth

Coons

My grandmother told me that farm house on White Creek
where Thelma Long lives with her five children is the place
my Mama and Daddy went to housekeeping.
Grandmother said she tried to help my Mama stay well,
she'd cook string beans and bring fresh cow's milk
in Mason jars for my sisters.

My Daddy tells it different. He says grandmother
was a meddler and they didn't need her mixing
in their affairs, poking in their business.

But even Uncle Charlie said Daddy was real mean
when he was liquored up. They all tell how he beat
Mama for hours in the upstairs the April she was
in her seventh month with me. Grandmother said I'd
be *marked*. "That baby'll be tetched," she said,
"and you'll be sorry; you'll get on your knees
and have to ask the almighty to forgive such wickedness."

Instead, Daddy moved Mama away from White Creek
and the pink roses she loved. After I was born,
he moved us clear to Ohio. That was before she gave
him two fine sons in eighteen months.

In West Virginia darkness, my grandmother rocked on her
porch and played *Amazing Grace* on the Jew's harp,
she told hundreds of sad stories about Mama's black eyes
and crying fits from Daddy's mean streak.

Daddy tells it different, he says Mama
had a sickness and having babies made it run from her
like sap from maples in the spring. That was before
he had his paralyzing stroke on the right side.

Grandmother told me coons only run so long in the night,
eventually, they'll tire and take a rest. And pretty soon
lathered dogs'll come, clawing crazy at the bark,
and all the men with their guns.

Delivery Men

They did not look
like our steel mill fathers,
those white-nailed men
who rang milk bottle bells,
smelled like incense,
lowered cardinal red flags
on hushed gray mailboxes.

They did not sound
like our steel mill fathers,
those honey-humming mailmen
and willow-whistling milkmen
who passed cool, sweaty bottles,
light bills, and sweet bird talk
to our melon belly Mamas.

They had tidy names
sewn straight
on their ivory soap shirts
right over the left pocket flap,
and crisp brown pant legs
buffed stallion black shoes.

They had racks
for clear, curved glass
and pouches for stamped letters,
and their names flashed
like medals in the sun.

And our gingham Mamas
smoothed floured aprons,
tucked stray hairs,
and June bride blushed
when they came — smiling,
every day —
delivering their parasol shade.

Desert Flowers

Their men took them to flat-footed milltowns.
Soft, doe-eyed mountain women and daisy haired
hillgirls said good-bye to their Mama's
wood-stove kitchen, their Daddy's clover fields,
and having babies at home.

Women who painted with needles said good-bye
to their granny's quilt frame. Hands that sliced
peaches and dishpans full of green beans
left blue canning jars — clean and silent —
in rows on cellar floors.

Their men said there was no fit place
for summer gardens, and these hillwomen hoped
there'd be a patch for tulips, prayed
there'd be a spot for apple trees.

When they came, the houses were shoe boxes,
air smelled worse than dirty sock haystacks,
iddy-biddy yards were cages where children
paced like tiger cubs, and cars were fleas
on the back of skinny, gray dog roads.

Our mothers were Saguaro cacti
learning to live without dancing clear streams
rushing down crying purple mountains, learning
to accept the mill's lattice of steel cables
and it's menagerie of mercury men.

Our mothers were Saguaro cacti
knowing they must turn brown to conseve water
so we, their daughters, could bloom.

Forty years later, we are their first arm.
Our daughters will be their second arm.
As both arms curve toward the breathless stars,

we will bury the placentas of their great-grandchildren
in the hills. We will give thanks to these beautiful women
who learned to survive the drought.

Thunder

Trees are half naked like crazy old men,
and a cool rain's coming down steady and hard
as Pauline Maxwell's *Amens* at August revival.

My baby brother's sucking his right fist
till purple spreads under his ivory skin
like berry stain. He's fussed for two days.
Now, he has no more voice for tears.

Mama's titties are dry as hard town dirt
since her last three shock treatments.
Doc Mason said our baby needs formula milk.
They sell it in cans with green labels
at Martin's Drug Store.

As if in a dream, Mama's a kite
without a tail, without a string,
blowing loose in our tiny kitchen.

Below her, clouds are thick with babies
and little girls tugging at her nightgown's
flannel hem, begging oats with brown sugar
or coffee bread for breakfast.

Mama empties the mayonnaise jar,
counts quarters, dimes, nickels.
She puts my oldest little sister, Mary,
in her rain bonnet and blue sweater.
*Go on now, that's a big girl, head up town
and buy this milk, what I wrote down
for baby brother. That's my big girl.*

Streetlights are ghosts in this rainy project
darkness, and Mary sets her lower lip
the way she does when our Mama's sick
and she don't want to cry.

Mary's bangs are hanging lickety-split
across her forehead. Out the screen door
she goes with Sam following her like a shadow
and wagging his dirty black tail.

It's a long way to town,
more than twenty ghost streetlights.
Now, it's raining harder than Preacher Smith
pounding his pulpit, and baby brother's fist
is about to bleed from hard sucking,
and green canned milk's sold only at Martin's,
and Mary don't have no boots, but Sam's beside her.
I reckon she'll be fine, long as it don't thunder
and Mama remembers brown sugar for my oats.

Paper Dolls

Ed Grimm thumps some on Alice Ray,
onlyest thing we can hear is her crying
through the bathroom screen.
I dress Betsy, fold tiny tabs over her shoulders,

around her waist, and a bonnet trimmed with lace.
Alice Ray sits in her green kitchen, one light overhead.
The night's black as the walls of our coal bin and heavy
as lard. Ed Grimm's holds his granddaddy's gun

to Alice Ray's soft yellow hair. My Daddy walks fast
up to Grimm's with Ted Wilson, and Mama calls us
in the house, our names break in the center like old saucers:
Mary, Benny, Davey, Nancy, Lee Ann.

After bit, Daddy and Ed and Ted sit on our side porch,
fill it up with their sprawling country-boy backs.
They pass a quart of warm home brew until it's gone,
smoke and chew and spit and cuss the mills.

If they were back home, it'd be bailing time, ice water'd
be carried in Mason jars to the wagons,
but here, in Ohio, it's lay-off season.
Pink slips are gunnysacks and men are kittens.

We bend together or fall apart,
like the dolls in my box.

Trains

Kathy's house was white, two-story
with black shutters, sat next to the tracks
and a patch of orange poppies.
When the trains came through, they grabbed
her house by its shoulders and shook it.
We felt our bodies tremble with those wheels.

Kathy, her sister, Rose, and I were shaking,
her three brothers rattled, her Mom's
breasts jostled, and Rebel barked softly.
Then Kathy would open one sable eye and say,
I really hate those damn trains.

But, I really loved those heading-somewhere-in-
the-night thunder trains. I imagined French-speaking
lovers kissing good-bye at moonlight stations.
I loaded cattle-smelling cars with stubble-faced men
whose sour breath played sweet harmonicas.

Lying beside my best friend, trains shaking
our covers, I dreamed a twinkling city filled
with goat herds, a sleeping hamlet at the ankle
of the sky, a city where love was a candle
burning in every window, a place where mothers
were pretty as poppies and children were butterflies.

I made a city that didn't breathe through
the nostrils of a steel mill, a town that didn't smell
like rows of slaughterhouse hearts,
a place where men could wrestle night to the ground
and drive their bursting lives as far as the brush
would paint, as far as the violin would cry.

Sunday Morning

Mama stands blotting her red lipstick,
and the tired Bible waits on our gray
kitchen table. We have a nickel
for the collection plate. We whine
because Ben gets to carry the nickel.
Ben will drop it, we say. Mama is firm.
We wear strawberry pink dresses, the boys wear
blue sailor suits. Bacon grease is Mama's scent.

Nancy scrapes cornmeal mush into Sam's bowl,
he gulps. Glass lies broken in the trash
and blood stains dry on our green couch.
Sunday morning means the end of Saturday night
pain. Mama buttons her aqua seersucker skirt.
She is a wave from the ocean. She presses
pancake make-up over her left shiner,
her ice bag sweats on the toilet.

My Mama sings softly beneath her wide-brimmed
straw hat, *Oh come to the church in the wildwood,*
and Mrs. Harvey points at my Mama, and the brown suit
preacher pounds his Methodist pulpit
screaming about hell's fury. . . .

My Mama's hair is the color of honey,
she quiets my brothers. My Mama's pancake make-up
melts from all this talk of hell.
Her left eye is a slit under a purple avalanche,
and purple is the color for the church,
the color for royalty.

Page Seven, Lee Ann's Baby Book

July 12, 1955

Willy Mackley welted your back with a stick.
I marched you straight to Sue's — welt
and tears and dirty knees.
Willy lied. Sue held him. You walloped
him right in the mouth. He won't forget
salty taste of his own blood. Sue and Myrtle
and I had lemonade about noon. We know
Sue did right. We don't hold with our boys
hitting girls.

Driving Lessons

Driving a car is the same as baking
cornbread, Mary Elizabeth. And I got
all the ingredients: gas, keys, this
beat-up Chevy, and a pair of sunglasses
so nobody'll know it's you.

I don't know, Martha Jane,
suppose Melvin finds out?

What's wrong with you Lizzy,
you've got to learn to drive.
That man, drunk half the time,
can't depend on him for anything
but another baby next May.

I never drove anything but
the tractor back home. Well,
once Melvin let me steer
his Ford truck at the drive-in.

Well today you are gonna shift
gears, push the clutch — hard honey,
all the way honey. Today, I show
you the beauty of idling, reverse,
and FORWARD. Put these shades on.
Go on now, put 'em on.

What about the baby?

You just fed him, and Myrtle
said the kids would be fine
with her. Hell, I'm teaching
her next week.

Myrtle's gonna learn to drive?

That's right, I told her she'd
pass her Ohio test — no hills here,
flat as a crew cut greased with *Brill Cream.*
She drove in Salt Lick, she can drive here.

How do I look?

Prettier than Patsy Cline
on a hot day with two black eyes.
Now Lizzy, just promise me you
won't ride the damn clutch.

I promise Martha Jane,
I promise.

Job Statement, 1950

found poem, Dorothy Burch
factory worker

When I first walked
in that plant
I had never had a job

outside my home,
and I thought
it was the biggest thing

I ever saw.
It was very menacing
to me, and the plant

doesn't have windows,
and having a background
from the farm,

it seemed
like I couldn't breathe.

The End of It

Tears and small faces press the screen door.
Two buttons are missing from Mama's rose print duster.
Daddy leads Mama to our blue Nash like an old mule
being drug to the fields. He's taking her back

to Woodside Hospital, that's where crazy people
have to go. First, Mama cries a few days, a few nights,
then we all cry for weeks. We must be bad. No one
else's Mama cries like ours. We try not to fight.

We flush. We wash up and lie quiet in our maple bed.
Davey's a bed wetter. Even with measles in July,
all five of us, we don't whine or dig. We wait for the end
of it. We watch Mama hang quilts over white windows.

Our granny told her what to do, said we'd
for sure go blind if she didn't. Sweat runs cricks
down the cracks of our butts. Now, Mama carries
wet cloths in a dish. Davey squirms, we slap him

to keep him still. We are vines. Rashes rub together,
itch spreads same as poison around an oak. In the night,
Davey forgets to wake up, warm piss hits my back cold
as May well water. I get my towel, dirty from the basket,

soak it up, pull off Davey's wet drawers.
Clean towels are in the closet. I can't reach them.
If I wake Davey, he'll just cry, and when he cries,
Ben starts. It's just that way with babies.

That starts Mama, she can't stop, not ever. Not even
with her yellow medicine or Preacher Smith laying hands
on her. *Her demons never go back to hell. Sweet Jesus.*
Our tick mattress is a flat rock, my nightie turns slowly

yellow, but I can't see none of this 'cause my Mama
hung quilts at blistered windows. She hates the darkness,

anything that hides the sun. All her babies got the big measles.
There's nothing to do but carry cool rags
and wait for the end of it.

My Grandmother's Engagement

I think we stand in the parlor, the room
that drapes over my shoulder like a hairpin shawl,
like a postcard fading inside a shirt box, like
a four leaf clover, dry and dying in a Bible.

The rose wool carpet's a lake there.
There is no boat, no moon, August shimmers.
The second hay swells in warm stacks,
a breeze rumples your hair, lingers where

I will bathe your neck years from now,
where your Sunday shirts will rub
under the striped ties, where our three sons
will squeal as you carry them to the barn.

What can I say? That your hair is parted and combed?
And my fences wait out there in your fields?
That light slides through them soft as weeds?
Shall I tell you your hands will cover me,

blind fingers reading a half-starved sea?
I have watched my mama, a tied quail,
thrusting scraps from her dishpan,
colorless, a glass of water in calico sleeves.

Shall I accept this ring you offer,
the soprano bells of a white church,
and find nothing to fill me beneath our
wedding quilts? A little more of nothing

each year? Shall I invent my turquoise oceans
and mountains rising while I toss corn to hens,
believe this life with you is the moon's roundness,
pink scent of honeysuckle at my feet?

Because, my love, even a wren can remember
the song bursting slowly inside them
above the wave's hammer, the wildness
of a drifting dream. Still, they fly to the cage,
grow gentle, touch what sand there is.

Madera Canyon
Walking With My Sister

No one believes walks are risky.
My sister's a house wren in a hot air balloon.
She has high blood pressure, says
It comes one day like a cold or measles
Never goes away.
Her white pills make her take chances
This May, she took me by the hand
High into Madera Canyon
See, she said, how cacti flowers blush
Purple fire from cool rocks,
Navajo women used prickly tips for needles.
She got straight A's in biology and history.
Today, we have no direction but up.
Mary Kay's hair blows hazel soft with canyon breeze.
She's flushed, and somehow, looks like our Mama
Gone these twenty granite years.
At this elevation, air is a whisper shared
In the dark, everything she points to turns
To gray trees leaned against each other,
Old ladies in floral dresses
Shuffling out of K-Mart on Saturday,
Saggy black pocketbooks
And scent of lilac perfume.
A blue light flashes and over my shoulder
The clearest stream I've ever seen splashes.
We are small again, running wet in warm grass,
The garden hose sprays a rainbow from Mama's hand.
We dance and hug each other in July mist,
Our Mama's voice a feather drifting down.
It comes one day like this,
Near the mountain's crest — it makes you choke,
It never goes away.

To Stop the Wind

Look into the wife's eyes
when she tells her story,
the one she's earned.

Her words are a woodpile,
their dog hit and still
by the weeds, her husband

sees it on his way home
from the mill, tells her
he must fetch his dog.

At the door, she calls
to him, *the dog is too heavy,*
and you are too old.

Against his chest, matted fur,
blood smell, flies kiss
the dog's split ribs.

She yells, *enough, enough.*
But, the man lifts his shovel,
walks to the shade.

Not by the pine tree,
by the maple, he starts.
She stands in the kitchen

peeling onions and crying.
She begs him to stop,
to wait for their son.

She wants him to rest,
to wash for dinner,
eat the brown roast on his blue plate.

But no, he says, the dog,
his friend, must be buried.
And so, it takes a long time.

He is old, the dog heavy.
He falls like coveralls,
wet and twisted in a basket.

Now, her words become
a thin blanket drawn tight
to stop the wind.

Her story's a chant
to raise him up, to chase him home,
bone of wish, leg of flesh.

Back, back, her hand pats
his forehead, combs his hair
as if he were a boy.

Her words are a neck
wrestling its chain.
Her tears are rain, and I am

a woman with open eyes.
I wince in this cold,
see my husband with his black dog

running, barking, even now.
One day, they will grow careless
and not see the truck's wheels.

Moth of wonder, this yoke of love.

And the hooves of the horses as they run
shake the crumbling field.

— Aeneid. Bk. xi, 875
Vergil

Pizza

I live in a small town.
When I order pizza
on Fridays — they know
my voice, realize my kids
hate hot peppers
and like extra cheese.

In the summer
our big events:
Fourth-of-July parade,
pee-wee baseball games,
and melting dreams of glory
from the edge of vanilla cones.

Our town has six churches
and twelve bars. We try
to save twice as many fiery
sinners in half the time
it takes to bury them
in our one graveyard.

Steel built our valley,
and even the links holding
our porch swings sound
like shackles
on the black ankles of night.

At dusk, middle-aged men jog
trying to overcome their silver
shadows, the phone rings
and a pretty girl with an Italian
last name says, *I know,
no hot peppers and extra cheese.*

In a small town, you can shower
before they slice your reality
into eight pieces.

Breeding

In the seventh grade we studied England,
learned about early coal mines,
children crouched in cramped tunnels.
Men bred horses to be tiny
so they could pull heaped coal carts.

I watched my father grow smaller
every summer at the mill,
until the only sound I heard
was his dapple phlegm
dragging dirty lungs up winter's hill.

Choosing Horses

found poem, J. F. Kelly,
horse dealer

When choosing a horse for foundation stock
I would look at the following points:

1. Height — fifteen hands or over.
2. Quality, balance and good general condition.
3. Ample bone below the knee and hock.
4. Sound, well shaped feet.
5. A deep, well-laid shoulder, capable
   of full extending the forearm.
6. A light, free mover, with great spring
   and elasticity.
7. Courage and boldness combined with a good
   temperament.

I would expect the stock from this cross to inherit:

(a) Jumping ability far above average.
(b) Flexibility and freedom of movement.
(c) Good temperament.
(d) Conformation and balance above average.
(e) Quality, bone and substance.
(f) Sound legs and feet.
(e) Strength and flexibility of hocks.

My Father's Pay Stub:
Rosedale Coal Company, February 15, 1941

For fifty-five hours at Rosedale No. 1
my father earned $41.17.
From that grand sum
they took $19.00 for the *store account*
and $.75 for *dues*
and $.50 for *assessments*
and $.50 for *burial fund*
and $1.50 for the *insurance*
and $.50 for the *doctor*
and $.41 for *F.O.A.*

His take home pay
for a wife with tuberculosis
and an infant daughter: $18.01.

After his wife passed,
father's mother, my grandmother,
raised the baby girl.

My grandmother saved buttons,
thread, and feedsacks
to make bonnets and dresses.

In 1979, the government
tried to deny my father's
Black Lung Benefits
because Rosedale's records
were gone, lost in a fire.

The Rosedale Coal Company
figured in everything
but my grandmother.

She lived to be ninety-five,
her attic piled with bins of blue jars,
cradles laced with webs.

three brown boxes
tied with butcher's string,
each one labeled for her sons.

Number One

It was the day for making the number one.
A white-haired woman walked around her first grade
classroom, and the girl in the blue dress drew
calligraphy *ones*: they had a curve on the left side
and a tiny base to stand on. The white-haired woman
stopped and said, "Make straight lines, that is not a *one*."

The girl in the blue dress had seen the curved
number one on a vitamin bottle in her Mama's hand.
She loved her Mama and the curve swooping up
like a bird and the base for the bird
to perch on. She made her page a tree filled
with soft swooping *ones*.

She was so busy drawing *ones* she didn't see
the hand coming to slap her across the face.
Diane Bailey turned and gave her a tissue.
Now tears were drowning her pretty *ones*.
The white-haired woman grabbed her *ones* paper
and crushed it with her slapping hand.

She handed the girl another sheet of paper.
Row after row after row the children's *ones*
lined up straight like bars across their pages.
The white-haired woman smiled.

A woman with brown hair sits at her writing table,
remembers her blue dress and hot tears.
She tells the story of ballerina *ones:*
they hold hands and dance and wear baby's breath
and satin slippers. Degas begs to paint them,
they refuse. They dance in leaves and snow and hay.
They dance and dance and dance. And when they grow
tired, they fly from her page like gray mourning doves.

Apple Chunks

I remember that day in the second grade
when I knew for sure my Mama'd never be well
enough to bring in orange juice and oatmeal cookies
for Halloween parties like Kathy Hawkins' Mama,
who had shiny gold hair and smiled all the time
like an angel on a Christmas card, 'cause my Mama
couldn't think to feed my baby brother or take her
yellow medicine or get herself out of her pajamas
before my Daddy came home from the mill.

And that's why Doc Mason said she'd have to be *committed*.
She'd been gone almost forever, and when I thought
about her, a chunk of apple caught in my throat.
I nearly couldn't breathe. Daddy divorced Mama
that same year. I reckon he was tired of her sickness.

In May, Aunt Hattie took a gall bladder attack,
and my cousin, Ruth Ann, showed her three stones
in a mustard jar. One was big as an acorn. And Luella
Donovan had a breast cut off for cancer (we never knew
which one), and Janet Porter's Mama had her female organs
removed when we were in the sixth grade.

All these women came home sickly pale from ether,
then one day you'd see them at the A&P
laughing by sack potatoes, their cheeks pink
as strawberry milkshakes. I don't figure my Mama
bought a slab of bacon by herself after I was nine.
I hated Doc Mason and my Daddy.

Last winter, Kathy Hawkins told me her Daddy died,
buckled up tight with a heart attack, which is easier
to take than brain sickness. I wrote her pretty Mama,
Mrs. Hawkins, a card and told her I was real sorry.
It is the hardest thing in life to chew gritty oatmeal
cookies and drink orange juice with apple chunks
stuck mean in your throat every bony day.

Coal Miner,
Caples, WV, 1938

Consider this coal miner, who is still young
and blue-eyed, how he rests his jaw
in timbers of his palm, face dusted over
with what most shafts exhale.

Down the road you know there's a shot hole,
the place where he drags his hope like a sledge
past the sun's pajamas, and pulleys lower
him in a wire basket.

Inside dark caverns, lessons begin.
His common hands follow glistening layers
of pigment to the middle ear of the mountain.
What does he hear in this immense labyrinth?

Does his heart complain that his shovel holds
no ruby, that air dances, a full-breasted woman
who spins her ether, drips juices over him,
a siren's song to make him stay?

He carries a silver pail, jam bread, yellow
cheese, coffee, cold in a jar, the memory
of screech owls in the hollows of his boyhood,
where he runs, fearless, and magnolias hang

in pink ruffles, warm yams stick to his fork.
He tastes all of this, smells brown manure
falling from his father's mules. His vision
persists, a grail filled with morning stars.

Think of the way we are all porters, the weight
of picks slung over our shoulders, leaving
in darkness, morning after morning, the shimming
up of our thigh bones to hold us in stanchions.

Isn't this it? The fatigue, days of garrets
furnished in quiet grumbles. Yet, we are rich
as this miner who scoops black honey
from a nettled ridge. We become the bear, rein
supreme in the starless land of tunnels,
where men with lanterns are kings.

Carrying the Kerosene
Coal Miner's Daughter, 1933

This is Pursglove, West Virginia
where the tipple's pyramid
announces something sacred's
taken from this valley.

Past ten steps and blind slats
lining the company store,
a miner's little daughter walks,
face down, dust soft as ribbons in her hair.

It's her turn to carry kerosene
for the lamps. She wears a white sundress,
dull brown shoes laced to her ankles,
the forwardness of meadow wildflowers.

With each step her weight bends
the grass, splits the tipple's shadow.
Ebony chunks swell like bread loaves
in rail cars bound for cities she will never see.

Morning glories are blue curtains
pinned to an abandoned porch.
They quiver and hang faded at the pane.
The child's life is a rustle in a dogwood's petticoat.

She'll outlive the tipple's empty belly,
the slack jaw of the ridge.
Beyond this moment, sense her breath,
warm as oven biscuits, her pink body

curled in a poster bed, her name:
Dreama, Dreama. When you are five
and your Mama calls, you hurry from quilts,
button your dress, risk details of early darkness,

green eyes of small animals, snorting of deer.
You fetch kerosene in a can, witness the miracle:
your father's brackened face
glowing, flawless, in the light.

Gray Fox

My grandfather's a gray fox in blue mountains.
He would never believe men walked on the moon
Trick photography, he said.
And he doesn't trust Medicare
When they issue checks, he refuses to cash them.
My aunts and uncles shrug their shoulders.
He lives in the same West Virginia basin
That his grandparents settled,
Watched his five babies be born, pink and screaming
In a two-window bedroom, carried warm placentas to his garden,
And felt sweet corn bulge heavy, then sprout gold tassels.
No one can make him buy life insurance
Or subscribe to the *Daily Press.*
When Walter Cronkite gave up on the nightly news
So did he.
He drilled water wells, raised pole beans like teepees,
And milked six cows as long as his eyes would let him.
Three sons fought in ugly wars and came home silent.
His 100 acres are posted with tiny yellow signs
That say *No Hunting*
Still, every season he has found white sheep
Or brown calves lying bloody in his fields.
When you stop to ask him where the road leads
He'll cut a plug of tobacco, spit once, and tell you,
Just about anywhere you've a mind to go.

Family Fiddle

I want to believe it traveled here
across an ocean, held by a poor boy
under his coat — Scottish or Irish —
someone hungry keeping it dry.

With very little effort prisoners
can be questioned. I examine first
the drab black case, its fasteners closed,
barely an inch of strap remains.

Shaped like a woman, the body's parched
and brown and quiet, the belly puffed
and empty. With both hands I lift it up,
slip the bow over four strings.

Before electricity, my people tell me
my great-grandfather played it for hours
on his evening porch, each note
a snowflake or star, the mist and blue dampness

you can only know if you've seen our mountains.
They say he cradled it so the ballads
became paintings, thatched roof houses,
gypsies dancing by their wagons.

I want to believe where we come from matters,
the past needs to be held and rocked
so every life's courage can be imitated,
the practice to get it right, embraced.

Mornings, the sun catches the slant of the slate roof
and the flanks of the young workhorses as they walk
the training ring with their black blinders in place.
The ring is a perfect circle of light. The horses
do not know how far they have to go before they can stop.
They do not know that they are going nowhere.
They do not know how their bodies take them there
but they do. The horses hear the whip and feel the blinders.
The dust spreads. Everything the horses leave behind,
the tracks they cover and recover, the white circle,
the morning light, palimpsest.

— *"Palimpsest"*
Maggie Anderson

The Story of My Village

Here is the story I write
about the men in my village,
my love for watching water.
The river was here first
and miles of hard road.
It is a small thing to believe
in order, believe in reaching.

My people came from blue mountains,
always the tribe sends men ahead
to build the fire. To describe this,
I must name our fathers: Clark,
Jenkins, Furriatti, who rose
with dawn, settled this valley.

Other men study oceans, handle
great nets, learn music of tides.
Because our river was here,
the steel mill came.
It isn't necessary to describe
its arms. I will say it cradled
our men, a poison wet nurse.

We were fragile and strange,
our men lost their language.
To describe this, I should name
their sickness: whiskey, wheezing,
tumors. Coils deafened; men grew numb.
They could not remember
the light of clear day.

One morning, big bosses inspected
our mill like Utah's desert
after the bomb tests — it was unfit.
They locked gates. To describe this,
I count what remains: ricocheting names

coughing in graveyards,
the thing that came first, our river,
and miles and miles of hard road.

Rank and File, 1959

*Most toxic substances have their origins in
the workplaces of America.*
Report, Ohio Environmental Council

Once hired, I became an apprentice
in survival. It hurts to breathe in here,
the air's metallic, and heat's a harness
rubbing every neck.

There are ways to suck the spirit
from people. How can you teach men
dignity and creativity when the boss
says, *make them dump the chemicals*

into the river on night turn?
So many fires. It's hard to tell friends
not to drink. But, in a steel mill
your physical life depends

on the right moves of other men,
and doing a good job's not enough,
the owners want it faster, cheaper,
more gold spun from mud.

Struggle never melts. Maybe because
my wife's pregnant, I dream water,
our son splashes, happy, warm, in the sink.
Bubbles. Bubbles. I have no impulse to change

the world, but all the men talk retirement,
how they'll *live then*, fishing, humping their wives,
making wine with their own grapes.
Every night we stampede to the time clocks.

Georgia wants a house, a garage, a picket fence.
This job may get them, get me. I'm union,
my hands know the give-and-take of grease.
We are a colony of men feeding one furnace.

We want the things we think are America:
forty hours, vacation, pension,
the right to live long enough to grow old
and not be wretched.

Homesick

Young men walked away from mountain velvet
to work Ohio's mills. Jobs were scarce
as hen's high heels back home, unless you settled
for the mines, let your lungs stiffen black with dust.

Josh and Luke moved into the far end of our house
two rooms and a bath, home brew in brown bottles,
and rag-tag kids to listen by their bare feet
while they hummed and remembered how blue

Kentucky grass grew, how salty West Virginia hams hung,
how Pennsylvania deer had bigger racks, and how they
missed watching stuff grow. Their hip pockets bulged
with Mail Pouch, like their jaws. They yearned to plow

a space and put down seed and wait for rain
and wait for green. Summer evenings, they'd pick
four-leaf clovers, show us the way slender grass
tight between your thumbs made a sweet whistle.

And the dirt of the mill ground deep, welded heat
from the shop made them thirsty. Weekends were not long
enough to get them back to Kentucky. Taverns were handy,
and liquor eased the fever for the plow.

Our Fathers

The day Joe Brodie fell into the acid pit
they say he screamed bigger than Texas.
When they pulled him out, his legs slid
off his waist like melted red candles.

He was crazy — screaming for his Mama,
his wife, Martha Jane, and his kids all at once.
Just before he blacked out, he clutched
his foreman's stiff white shirt and said,

Help me Tom, please . . . my legs.
Joe Brodie died on the way to the hospital.
Our fathers finished their shift.
That night, my Dad and his best friend, Ted,

went to Tony's Bar and got slop-the-hogs-
falling-down drunk. They talked about school days
back in Bobtown, PA and how yeast dough
smelled rising in their mamas' kitchens,

how many bales they could toss in June,
and how they missed those sweet, lazy
West Virginia nights, and how hot Ohio was,
hot and flat, and people here called us *hicks*

and *ridge runners*, but by God, we knew
how to work. And our fathers never missed a shift.
Salt stains scribbled lines on coveralls
like small boys print their names in dirt.

Definition of a Blast Furnace

found poem in brochure
Ohio steel mill

A giant retort
used by the steel industry
for making iron

in which 2,758
competing reactions
are taking place

simultaneously —
all, more or less
out of control.

Mileage

A few years near the blast furnace
and every guy looks alike.
                    Thomas Geoghegan

Father had an eighth-grade education,
he'd worked the coal mines, didn't loathe
boxy darkness of our small garage,
where after his shift and before supper
men brought their cars:
the milkman's sedan, Ramblers, Chevys,
dying Fords driven by his union brothers.

After a full day, lying down is hard,
a barn with no heat, a father,
his door always closed, a smithy
in carbon-monoxide apron
fitting brakes like shoes
to the rim of hooves. They paid
him a little at a time.

He never whistled or hummed,
but studied the black congestion
beneath each hood, an old midwife,
he felt the gush of warm fluids
settle like blood on his shirt, trousers,
and shoes. Behind vapors, his wrench
pawed heater hoses, partial rot of fan belts.

Here was the muddled space of living
below the surface, cells bound with conflicting
loyalties. It's clearer now why he kept
a bottle hidden in his shop rags,
rain to wet the brown leaf's membrane,
a needle to ease the pain of fixing
another's trouble, something to dull
the thought of wanting the jack to fall.

The Main Man

Below heaven's arch
the mill's catwalk strewn with petals,
ore pellets the color of ox blood.

Under old steel beams
the raspy sermon
of our blast furnace operator.

He coughs and shakes
his fist at hell. His blue shirt clings
to his chest, a soaked baptism robe.

Here, his life and coffee
are dark and still
growing cold in white styrofoam.

They cannot be born again.

Operations

On the second floor of the mill
there's a sign above one door:
RECOVERY ROOM
as though someone's had surgery
and now, they're sleepy
from all the gas
still hurting
whenever they move or cough.

The Devotion of Brown Lives

As much as anything
the song of men pressed together
making steel
is a miracle in this valley.

See the warm bars quiet down
stacked careful, and cooling.
They are red candles in our grotto.
These brothers want to believe

their lives are more than a magnet
dangling from chains, traveling
back and forth like a gray sun
to eat the scraps of what stays piled.

I think how language
starts with screams, then tears,
how men learn early to wait
their turn at the fountain.

Tonight the shift whistle
has a rhythm of bells,
and light from the furnace
is a smokehouse in a village

where everyone works,
and the men don't hate their houses
in the distance or the spaces between them
blessed with trees.

The Field's Red Wheat

If you follow any river far enough
you'll find a locked country
expresses no emotion, and it's better
sometimes to forget the mandolin and fiddles,
how your people would clap and dance
after the harvest, how they tied flowers
and ribbons on the cows, how your mother
embroidered your sister's blouse.

Men who worked beside my father
at the steel mill carried their names
strapped to their backs like bundles of sticks
or a sack of damp potatoes, something
they might boil and eat or use to start a fire.

Balducci, Liptak, Batarovich, Behun,
men who lived on Hunky Hill
knew the attics' steamer trunks had a job
sending signals of silence into space
where the past was a root cellar.

How much English did they learn?
How much did they understand?
Father never asked. Questions were a gate
to a pasture where a man needed permission
to enter, and he didn't have the words.

The men were glad for any shift and weekend
overtime, they had a cousin, their wife's brother,
they want come, they want work in America. America.
On hot ingots they warmed pirohi, holupki,
balls of summer sausage.

If the mill was anything
it was a tent for the hungry, and memory
was the valley left behind

where they'd seen the field's red wheat,
and the grapes' faces grew dusty blue,
their sweet bodies waiting to be crushed.

The Mill's Annual Picnic, 1960
Conneaut Lake Park, PA

Try this. Try saying your father looked natural
in his purple Hawaiian shirt and khaki bermudas,
legs pale as bedsheets for that July day every summer
when the town packed up early, left
to claim a good table under red pavilions.

On that day, the mill treated us to ferris wheels
cutting the sky with pink neon lights,
cotton candy, helium balloons on a stick.
Twirl around the merry-go-round on the black horse,
reins slack, watch your father tie those white tickets
to your sisters' wrists, your brothers' belt loops,
tell you all to stay together, hold hands,
carry the iced tea, hot dogs, mustard and buns.

Stand beside him, squinting in the open field,
sun carving his shadow over the family like a mountain,
huge orchids dizzy in his sleeves
while his union president cracks dumb jokes,
spins a wire hopper to pull lucky numbers,
an electric skillet or steam iron,
something to make your mother's life easier.

Watch his buddies, Howard, Joe, and Ted,
their eyes are hard and dry and stubborn.
Watch how they walk, apart from sundressed wives,
their fingers, used to cables and steel coils,
fumble diaper bags and baby bonnets,
squeeze the strollers' metal handles.

Remember how after lunch, your father drifted
to the bar near the lake, and its dark wood
softened the lavender in his shirt,
and the sour smell of liquor made him smile?
How easily he mounts his stool,
grabs the thick mane of sad music,
buries his face in the haze.

Art in the Mill

From the beginning you must believe
it hammers in silence and has its own
routine of faith, even the smell of a cigar

might become a poem or a man's reflection
in his lunch pail wearing a hard hat
cast some light. Because a flannel shirt

draws warmth from a man's trunk,
you must acknowledge his soul possesses fire.
In the kingdom of coveralls, you have to imagine

pines, a forest where it is Sunday forever,
a clearing so full of morning, you want to pray.
There's nothing wrong with pretending ore pellets

are grapes ready for dancing feet or a huge vat.
Communion flowers everywhere.
Because a tow motor is the exact yellow

of mustard seeds, you must pay attention to the fields.
Because art whispers you must listen and trust your eyes.
One Tuesday, I visited a steel mill, a rare thing today,

all the men seemed hopeful,
their hands and faces
were covered in sculptor's dust.

How to Say It

Pronounce it *mill*
let your lips mash together until they hurt,
exhale the *i* sound, then your tongue
licks the seam of your incisors.

Wasn't this word the center of your valley,
the loading docks, blast furnace, smokestacks
five times higher than your grandfather's barn?
Wasn't this world filled with salty men

like your father, buttoned in greasy coveralls,
laced in scorched boots? Didn't these men pull
raw coils like bloody newborns
from the labia of the rollers?

If you look at your own hands, do you see
your father's blisters and black creases,
places where gray days slipped into his lifelines
and cables became nails in his palms?

Aren't there two ways to spell *steel*?
And doesn't one of them mean something's
been taken away? Something unspeakable.
Listen, I want to tell you those smokestacks

were five times higher than my grandfather's barn
and men build what they believe is real
because work is the cross they carry,
and even cutting off their arms
won't make them put down their tools.

Snow Horses

It's about a mountain
where the sun did not wear goggles,
and the river's breath was blue,
a meadow where mothers dance —
gypsies in lavender skirts — children's
laughter floats like blown dandelions.

Here are the magic stars above
the fathers wheezing up the mountain.
Without a sound fingers bloom, sleeves unfold
lost arms, legs fill pinned trousers. The men run —
pale and glistening — their boots are hooves.

When they reach our mothers, their shirts are gone.
On bare backs they hoist us: women, babies, children.
They sprint past the line of pyramid pines, through
the patch of blue flax, the moon's an ivory ball
and we toss our arms back to catch it.

They race: nostrils, manes, tails flying
to the top of a mountain that never was, though I dreamed
a space for it and understood — how light heals men.
Tell everyone I was there with the others, holding on,
riding our snow horses.

Nothing disturbs them now. In slow increase
They fatten like the grass. Doomed to be idle,
To haul no cart or wagon, wear no bridle,
They grow into a vegetable peace.

— *"Horses"*
Jorge Guillén
translated by
Richard Wilbur

Release of the Spirit

Even if we say the lives of ordinary people
may be the dandelions blooming, coming
always back, year after year,
who will believe us?

We are the children raised in a town
at the bottom of the ocean, an ocean
which was never named, and our mill
was a Spanish galleon destined to go down.

Wasps humming in the guard shanty
are the kind voices of workers on the job,
they let the sun pass through trembling
on its knees. Is it wrong to lift a lantern,

to search what's left of the wreck?
Things keep calling us: the parking lot's
gray face where wind fingers the grass
like a widow counting her pension —

thin, green bills — and rows of steel dies
sit mute, old men in robes above a chess board.
How can we write the story of such a journey
with anything but blue ink?

We have signed a contract with a no-strike clause.
Even if we claim there were no hard times
or hunger or fear of tomorrow,
who'd believe us?

We are the children whose fathers learned
the world is flat
after work there's nothing,
but the heart's quiet roar.

Settlement

*"This was the place where the galleon was wrecked
and the horses swam ashore."*
Fishermen, Assateague, VA

Not the storm's rage or the sailors' fear.
No. Not even the stolen gold coins locked
in trunks. Not the ropes or torn sails.
Not the cries to heaven above the flailing.

Forget the log's language, the salted flesh
packed in barrels. When the ship's ribs split,
the moon was present, and metal lattice
used to close the floor rose, no slaves

below, just horses, a small calvary being swallowed
by the sea, gasping, confused, kicking to come up,
to breathe. Air, air, finally, and the cool darkness,
God's black hand turns them away from the wreck.

The unburied say: *Everything seemed gray,
you maintain position, don't want to fall behind,
something, maybe your heart, swells at the front
of your neck. It pulls you from earth's stratum*

to a city of sea grass, a country of sand.
No provisions. No master.
Gone are the bit and bridle, the quiet shelter
of a barn. The only weight

upon your back's the sun, the rain,
the season between winter and summer.
What shall you do, beautiful, shaggy horses
with this death you have survived?

Lourdes

Where be all his miracles
which our father told us of?
                    Judges 6: 13

There were rumors:
if the men took pay cuts,
gave up sick time and vacations,

shaved some insurance benefits,
our mill might be spared.
We waited for a sign.

The blessed mother did not appear
on the project playground,
and when Mrs. Cavelli cut her palm

slicing pepperoni, Father Conko shook
his head, said that wasn't really *stigmata*.
Round the clock women in babushkas

prayed the rosary. Candles burned
in rows at St. Michael's and St. Joe's.
All that smoke and incense,

still, not one statue wept.
At the union hall, some of the men
came drunk, cursing. My father (who never

spoke before a crowd) stood up:
Don't give the sonsabitches nothing back,
we worked too damn hard to get what we have.

Let the bastards close her down.
We waited for a sign.
The next day they hung it on the gate.

Piecework

When times are bad, you can do it at home.
The pay's low, but hunger's a good thing to know,
to remember. Plant your garden even if the bombs
are coming. Take shit from no man.

Be a rag sorter, follow the horse-drawn carts
with two wheels. Faith is the main thing.
Carry hope on your shoulders like a saint
for feast days. Mix Dago red in the coffee

for nights of picket duty, a decent wage is worth
the beating. Slow down, sit down, walk out
on any speaker who says, *you have no right to go back.*
When you grieve, take the person with you:

your father, mother, the forty-year-old woman
who died paralyzed from working too close
to the freezer all those months
in the bacon-finishing department.

She had kids. Be willing to go to jail for an idea
about justice. A log driver says to loosen a jam's
dangerous, it can cause death, but a stopwatch
can be a gun, and a man is not a machine that works.

Don't forget the last days, your father
and the men stood around the gate
singing labor songs, wondering
what they'd do tomorrow.

Where Animals Gather

Six black metal cranes stand apart
in gravel fields, where snows of memory
are deep. Giraffes waiting for ginseng
and green umbrellas to burst forth,

tireless lettuce from treetops. Unable to cry, rain
drizzles down ebony chins, braids itself
into puddles under their hooves. Unthinkable
to imagine these charcoal bodies

moving endless and forceful and sure
shift upon shift, autumn after autumn, holding
our mill's promise like a candle, lifting up,
sustaining, swallowing.

Push this gate, dear reader, nothing here
is typhus or smallpox pus or a madman with a gun.
Here, steel cranes are giraffes, black bones leaning,
and men are geldings, voiceless in gales.

This is the lake of frozen dreams
where sunsets stagger, where animals gather
in half-moon circles to chant the bitter taste of rust
and sweet mercy of bullets.

Another Abraham
For My Father-in-Law, John, Who Worked at the Mill

Today your sons gazed at the pasture's fresh calves
and told their story again. They are fourteen
and fifteen, dressed like James Dean
sneaking smokes behind the garage, lying about girls
and using rubbers. Their voices are mist, then fog.

Every time they tell it, it's the rain pushing them
back inside childhood's faded house.
Boredom makes them wrestle. They fall
upon the maple bed, slats ache, then break.
Who ran first for the coffee can filled

with roofing nails, they cannot say.
But, they hurried to fix the bed you could not
afford to replace. Boys love secrets.
And brown shoe polish covered broken cracks
like dried blood. For a few days, things held.

Then, one night, without warning, their weight
collapsed the wooden frame. Across the darkness,
they heard your sleepy voice, *What happened?*
Together they lied, *We don't know Dad;*
we were just sleeping; the bed fell down.

What did you know, John? You were a farmer's son
sent to war, and then, a boss at the steel mill.
Did you know how soon they'd leave the gauze
of summer's sheets? Did you see them growing old
in a steel town covered with the dust of their lives?

Oh breath, oh labor of the father and the sons.
Did you stand there fearing the knife in your pocket
and the table which consecrates bread and wine?
Even then did you believe what your life's angel
whispered? You'd take these boys, your fine sons
to learn the mill's language of *graveyard* and *slitter.*

Because family stories fall away like leaves,
I wanted you to know when they tell it, they remember
the forgiveness, and how, for a while things held.
In their voices you can hear something tangled:
an aching to go on, an aching to stop.

The Valley of Steel Mills

My husband and I live in a small house
in Ohio near a farm, the meadow grows fat
with hay, the cows swell with milk,
the white fences are everywhere.

Each harvest has its price.
My husband has twenty-five years
with General Motors and with me. I don't know
which occupation is the most work,

a wife with dreams of poetry or factory life.
I think that the building of cars is very difficult work,
the plant is very hot in the summer, very cold in the winter,
the work is dirty, dangerous, and it deafens.

I watch him and I see our fathers in the steel mill,
their faces glowing near the furnace,
their eyes brilliant with something like tears.
The men understand weight and whirlwind.

Life inside the corral is one of patient duty,
the whip is silent and slow and sure.
I think that love is the whip we cannot see
and every day my husband buries his dreams

for the good of his family. Each year he has less
energy to break and run, he hears less and less the melody
of his boyhood music. In this valley, the women learn
to love the dust because whatever is buried here is truly sacred.

The Human Thing

The sun disappears when we enter the barn.
I am five, maybe six and marvel at her
soft, willing hands on the teats.

Their bags are full, fingered pink balloons.
No other sound in the stable except
squirt-slosh, squirt-slosh against the metal pail.

Work looms everyday: hinges, hooves,
ropes pull toward a stanchion.
The need for money to repaint the house.

For morning's labor, my grandmother straddles
the stool, apron's gauze a kitten in her lap.
I am not clear about kitchen boilers

or the process of milk and whey heated
or how long it takes curd to set.
But I understand her bonnet's calico

hemmed in silence, the cycle of taking milk,
turning the baby in a mother's arms,
the human thing I've seen with my brother's

tongue and Mama's breasts, the purr of gentility.
All around us gray stalls, cow smell, and love
for a life that does not pay.

Tonight, years past the woman and the girl, beyond
father's boyhood farm, a hospice nurse
traces father's brow, minds his morphine.

His breathing crackles like trampled straw.
My sisters hug, brothers pace the room
like hired help sick of this idleness.

Language searches for what's been lost.
The last day, when even a sheet's lightness
was too heavy, father said *milk*. The urinal was *milk*;
his glasses were *milk*; our names were *milk*.

Caught in the foaming, I stood there
while his entire body drew it well into his mouth,
and bonnet flowers on his gown
bloomed small, bloomed small, bloomed small.

Why It Happens

I sit down on my blue glider to read Hemingway as my neighbor's wife, Susan, makes her fifth pass in the wheat field. Her combine's a chariot and she's a goddess, long yellow hair French braided down her back. She drives this giant machine the way guys named *Stitch* and *Blade* ram Harleys. If she knew I was here, sipping iced tea by my barrel of red geraniums, she'd wave.

She's dressed like a waitress at Joe's lunch counter, as well she might be coming from a steamy kitchen to take another order for fries and BLTs. In the windowed cab of the green machine, she holds her toddler daughter, Jenny, on her lap. Thrust and thrum of vibrating earth and gnawing grain shimmies through their warm thighs. What is it they share in this hazy space? Row after row of sunlight, riding this neck of growling dinosaur, do they sing above its grinding smell of grease? Does the child learn the many gears of silence?

Because I'm selfish, I moved to the country. I love the bouquet fragrance of new mown hay and watching lazy dirt trail farm tractors. I enjoy this without rising early for the fields. I can witness this without ordering spring seed and fretting over rainfall and hail storms. Clouds are white elephants to me. I work where air conditioners keep my mascara lines straight.

And when calving times comes, Susan invites us over to the barn. I take my daughter to see stalls convulse with blood and placentas and bawling. I explain biology cycles, birth, why it happens like it does, why it looks so messy. All the while, Susan holds Jenny astraddle her left hip, black rubber boots half stuck to straw, a dim light shines on their golden hair. Susan chews a piece of Juicy Fruit. Jenny smiles, sleepy on her mother's shoulder. They are not listening to me dwell on the delivery. The calf has started to get up: glistening, buckling, wet with her life.

Under a Funeral Canopy in Rockingham, NC

for Chris Llewellyn
and all those who study ashes.

Seventy-five miles southeast of Charlotte, North Carolina
and eighty years past window fragments of The Triangle
Shirtwaist Company in New York, women still stampede,

fall through each other in smoke filled rooms, faces grow black
like gangrenous limbs. In this photograph, Kenny Jarrell strokes
the slick hard top of his Mama's cool casket. He is lanky,

about eighteen, wears charcoal shades and a paisley tie.
I wonder if his eyes are blue. Over his top lip, his first
moustache, in his right arm, a pretty girl, Annette Williamson.

Bertha: Kenny's Mama's name, a name stronger than memory.
She worked day shift at the chicken-processing plant in Hamlet,
North Carolina. Seventeen women and seven men perished in the blaze

with Bertha. Flames under fryers ignited the mist that set
fire to the shirts that touched the soft hair that made open
mouths scream and frantic hands tug at gold knobs while backs

cowered and crawled, skin blistered and broke, over spasms and coughs,
palms beat drums against doors, sclera raw as the flames. Tears slid,
prayers slipped from nonbelievers' lips as they pried on steel doors,

the solid doors still being locked on America's workers.
Foremen feared chicken nuggets might go home in purses
and lunch pails. Most of these women were single parents.

Children will arrive like sad letters in the mail to foster homes,
relatives who do not know they hate onions, have trouble
with long division. One firefighter was cut, fifty-four workers

burned or treated. Royal Food Products ordered pink roses,
white daisies, yellow mums to douse the stench of charred flesh.
And the overflow of bodies went to neighboring towns like muddy

rivers swollen in spring rains. Some victims were too crisp
for fixing up. Bertha Jarrell's box is ornate, Roman column edges
and inlays march straight down the sides. Fancy, every inch fine

and fancy. Mayor Amy Carrington's scratching her head
and says, *This isn't the kind of thing you bargain for. . . .*
The Baptist preacher nods, and the governor will surely

look into it. And Kenny Jarrell agrees, beneath his silent
white shirt, his heart beats, a red fist on his left side, the side
he presses against his Mama's brilliant white coffin.

Blue Collar

You must change your life.
Rilke

We know, we surely must know
there are moments before explosions,
before any body count, when breaking
windows and screaming might have helped.

Serious bargaining over the old contract:
human dignity and ruling by fear.
No simple answers exist,
but when they tell you, *They got greedy;*

see, now it's gone, it's all gone.
What they really mean is, *it's OK*
to let some furnaces go cold,
some children go hungry.

Did your teachers ever make you memorize
the names of coal strikes? steel leaders?
tell you the story of the Triangle Shirtwaist Company?
the chicken factory in Hamlet, NC?

Learn the Gettysburg Address,
the Pledge of Allegiance,
the Preamble to the Constitution;
study hard, and you may move up, they said.

But the rules are the rules,
justice doesn't wear a flannel shirt.
Without the working class,
what is America? What is America?

Where are the great studies on buried miners,
burned women, displaced steel workers,
the lost towns gutted like deer,
people left to choose between the river and the sky?

Anything Is Possible

You can make the story different,
the smooth tires abandoned in the lot
— where your house was —
they can be your brothers' church shoes

shined and waiting to be laced.
So what if the mailbox is gone?
Let the pine tree be mama's green couch,
those two beer cans, doilies for each arm,

that covey of pebbles, baby teeth
swapped for nickles in the night.
Let the curved puddles of water
be your sisters whining when knots

were brushed from their wet hair.
Move from the center outward — see,
the coal furnace becomes less grumpy,
and your father's blue cigarette haze

is a white candle lit for absolution.
Go slowly, reading every sign for pardon,
the unraked leaves are kittens wrestling,
the found nest, a first birthday cake,

the wet newspapers, oval throw rugs drying
on the line, high in the maple's branches
those caught stars are Davey's kite,
the moon, a cup of cold milk and your mama

saying, *Nat King Cole is all over his cancer;
I'm so happy.*

Notes

"The Mill's Annual Picnic, 1960, Conneaut Lake Park, PA" was performed at Cleveland State University July 1998 in the Mirror of the Arts Program *Growing Up:Persons, Places, Things*; "Delivery Men" was performed at the Cleveland Art Museum June 1996 in the Mirror of the Arts Program *Cityscape*; "Sunday Morning" was performed at SPACES, Cleveland, Ohio in 1992 Mirror of the Arts Program *Unresolved Grief.*

"Desert Flowers" is dedicated to my mother, Wilma Stiles Henderson, "The Human Thing" to my father, Willis B. Henderson, and "The Valley of Steel Mills" to my husband, David. The following poems are dedicated to the men and women who work at Warren Consolidated Industry in Warren, Ohio, with special thanks to my friend, Bob Mazur, for arranging a tour of the mill, Bob Moss for conducting it, and Richard Mokros for granting special permission for this valuable experience. The following poems are a direct result of that journey: "The Main Man," "The Devotion of Brown Lives," "Operations," "Definition of a Blast Furnace," and "Art in the Mill."

After attending the 1997 **Working Class Lives and the Future of Work** conference at Youngstown State University, I wrote the following poems: "Rank and File, 1959," "Mileage," "Settlement," and "Blue Collar." I am convinced that listening to the presentations of Janet Zandy and Tillie Olsen guided the creation of these poems. I thank them and the organizers of the conference.

"The Valley of Steel Mills" was written first for a Spanish class assignment from Dr. Ron McCrary. For this manuscript, I chose to use the English translation. The following poems were written after photographs of Marion Post Wolcott, a photo journalist, who worked for the Farm Bureau Agency during the depression: "Carrying the Kerosene, Coal Miner's Daughter, 1933" and "Coal Miner, Caples, WV, 1938."

Sources

Bornstein, Jerry. *Unions in Transition.* New York: Simon and Shuster, 1981.

Boryczka, Raymond, and Lorin Lee Cary. *No Strength Without Unions.* Columbus: Ohio Historical Society, 1982.

Geoghegan, Thomas. *Which Side Are You On?* New York: Farrar, Straus and Giroux, 1991.

Kelly, J.F. *Dealing With Horses.* New York: Arco, 1961.

Lynd, Alice and Staughton. *Rank and File.* Boston: Beacon, 1973.

Scott, Jack Denton, and Ozzie Sweet. *Island of Wild Horses.* New York: Putnam, 1978.

Jeanne Bryner was born in Waynesburg, Pennsylvania, in 1951, and lived in West Virginia until age four. Summer visits to her grandparents' farms in West Virginia and Pennsylvania instilled a love for blackberries, barn smells, dailiness, and the sweet muslin of stories told in porch darkness. Growing up in the projects in an Ohio steel mill town where production meant new shoes or no shoes or last year's shoes taught her how lives are shaped by work.

A graduate of Trumbull Memorial Hospital School of Nursing and Kent State University's Honors College, she has won several awards for community service, nursing, and writing. To facilitate the healing power of language, she teaches writing workshops in cancer support groups, schools, nursing homes, and universities. She has received fellowships from Bucknell University for the 1992 Younger Poets Seminar, the Wick Poetry Program at Kent State University, and the Ohio Arts Council in 1997. Her poetry has been adapted for the stage and performed in Ohio, West Virginia, Texas, Kentucky, New York, and California. Her first collection of poems, *Breathless,* was published in 1995 as part of the Wick Series by Kent State University Press, selected by Maxine Scates.

She lives near a dairy farm with her husband, David, their daughter, Summar, and a sixty-two pound boxer. Her son, Gary, lives in southern Ohio with his wife, Lisa. Jeanne is an emergency room nurse and a poet.